q is always followed by u.
The letter q borrows the sounds of K and W.

You never write    always

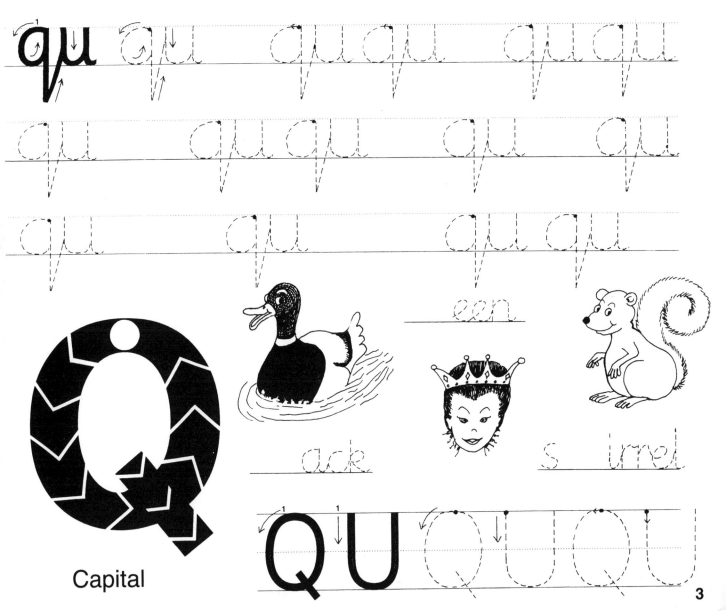

q u

qu   ququ   quququ

qu   ququ   qu   qu

qu   qu   ququ

een

ack

s__irrel

Capital

Q U   QU ququ

"Ou!" cried the girl. "I've pricked my finger with the needle."

ou

Action: Pretend your finger is a needle and prick your thumb saying *ou, ou, ou*.

4

Write your name.

QU
qu

On sunny days Inky, Snake and Bee go to see the ducks.
Inky pretends her paws are a beak and shouts *qu, qu, qu*.

Action: Make a duck's beak with your hands and say *qu, qu, qu*.

ouch ouch

Copy

our

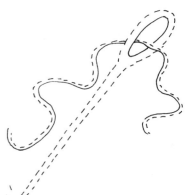

ou   ou ou ou   ou ou ou

ou ou ou   ou ou

ou   ou ou   ou

h__se

d__d

m__th

Read the words

count
• • • •

round
• • • •

shout
• • •

oi

"Oi!, ship ahoy" shouted the captain of the ship.

Action: Cup hands around mouth and shout as if to another boat, *oi!, ship ahoy!*

oi! ship ahoy!

Copy

oi

oi oi oi oi oi oi oi oi

oi oi oi   oi oi oi

oi oi oi oi   oi oi oi oi

OIL

p_nt

b_l

Read the words

coin
● ● ●

joint
● ● ● ●

spoil
● ● ● ●

7

ue

Inky, Snake and Bee are playing 'Guess Who?'
When the music stops they guess who has the
ring, pointing and saying *ue*.

Action: Point to people around you and say *you, you, you*.

ue is the last vowel sound. Watch out!

 ue

ue ue ue ue ue ue

ue ue ue ue

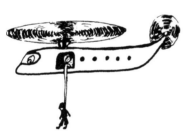

resc_____

barbec_____

There are two other ways to write the *ue* sound.

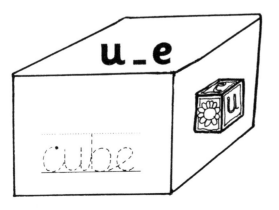

u_e

cube

ew

ewe

9

Inky is making some gingerbread people.
She mixes up all the ingredients with a
mixer - *erererer.*

er

Action: Roll hands over each other like a mixer and say *erererer.*

Instructions

For making The Bad Tempered Goat book.

1. Take out the 2 middle pages of your workbook.
2. Cut and separate the 2 pages and place one on top of the other.
3. Cut along the dotted line marked with scissors.
4. Put the 2 pieces on top of the others. Keep the title page at the front. Check your page numbers.
5. Fold to make your book.

16

The Bad Tempered Goat

To Bee from Snake.

1

Then he butted the trunk of the oak tree.

12

He used to shout very loudly,

and butt his horns against the tree trunk when he was angry.

5

Farmer Brown has lots of animals on his farm.

2

It was a Monday morning and Farmer Brown was feeding his animals.

6

The goat felt very silly and promised never to be bad tempered again.

15

The goat got very angry.

He ran up and down.

11

He was stuck.

Farmer Brown had to get out his
tractor to help the goat get free.

14

He has rabbits pigs cows horses
chickens and a goat.

3

Then he flew down and sat on
the goat's horns.

10

He had just given the goat a big
bag of oats ... when ...

7

The goat had a very bad temper.

4

crack! creak! crunch!

He butted the tree so hard that the tree fell on top of him.

13

... a cheeky robin took a quick mouthful and

flew up to the lowest branch of the oak tree.

8

"Good Morning," he shouted down to the goat.

9

gingerbread

gi _____

er er er er er er er er

er er er er er er

er er er er

mix

g m

dinn

Read the words

winter
• • • • •

summer
• • • •

sister
• • • •

ar

The girl has a very bad sore throat. The doctor makes her say *ah.*

Action: Open mouth wide and say *ah,* as if at the doctors

Mind the sharks to reach the chart.

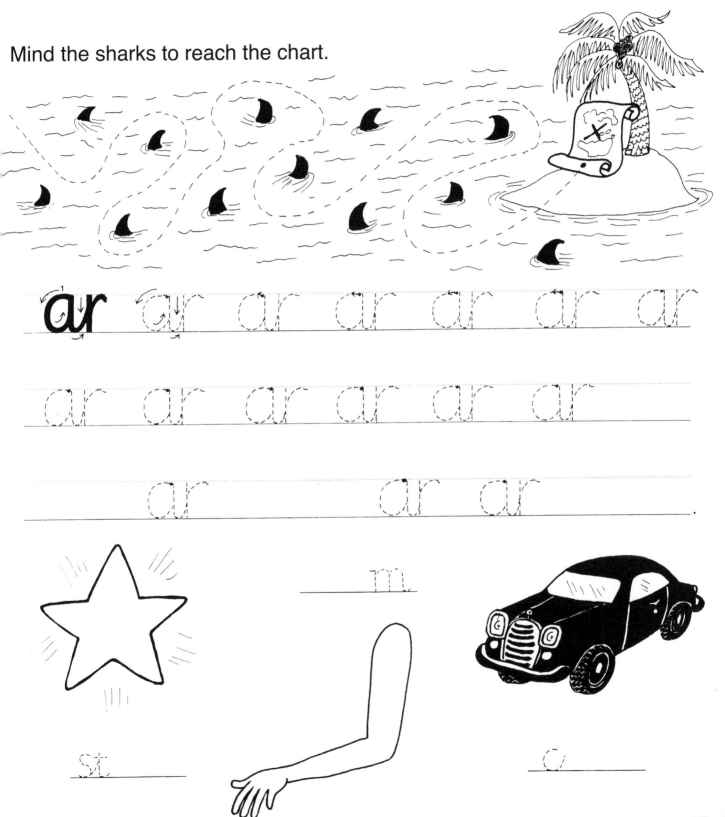

ar ar ar ar ar ar ar ar ar ar ar

ar ar ar ar ar ar ar ar ar ar ar

ar ar ar ar .

st____ m____

____ar

Practice of the o and w shapes.

ou

ow

owls

Wordsearch

oi **oy**

t	o	y	a	f	c
d	p	o	i	n	t
p	e	k	v	z	j
c	o	i	n	g	o
h	r	u	b	o	y
o	i	l	m	q	s

oil   coin   boy

point   toy   joy

Choose the correct 'er'.

er ir ur

g _____

c _____

w _____

Read each word and draw a picture of it.

ou ow

mouth

cow

brown

clown

owl

cloud

crown

house

mouse

21

Write a sentence about each picture.

The number 7

1 2 3 4 5 6 7

7

seven   seven   seven

In this last book in the series, the numbers eight and nine have been included.

1 2 3 4 5 6 7 8 9

8 8 8 8 8 8 8 8

eight   eight   eight

9 9 9 9 9 9 9 9

nine   nine   nine   nine

Activity

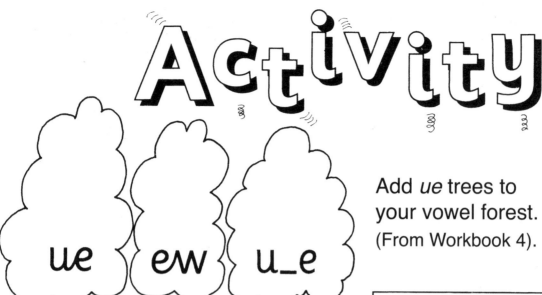

ue ew u_e

Add *ue* trees to your vowel forest. (From Workbook 4).

Make a star and clouds picture.

Collect *ar* words to go in the stars and *ou* words for the clouds.

Make some gingerbread people.
Decorate them with currants or icing.

Ouch!
Read the story of Sleeping Beauty who pricked her finger on a needle.